The Chemistry of Economic Growth

By Kevin S. Crowder, EDP

Collision Theory in Practice

Copyright © 2024 Kevin S. Crowder

All rights reserved

No part of this book may be reproduced, or stored in a retrieval system, or transmitted in any form or by any means, electronic, mechanical, photocopying, recording, or otherwise, without express written permission of the publisher.

BusinessFlare® Publishing Group

Cover design by Lina M. Duque

Printed in the United States of America
ISBN: 9798303213876

CONTENTS

Forward 1
Introduction: The Chemistry of Economic Growth 4
Chapter 1: A Chemist's Legacy 9
Chapter 2: Activation Energy: Overcoming Barriers to Progress 13
Chapter 3: Catalysts: Igniting Economic Growth 19
Chapter 4: The Dynamics of Successful Collisions 25
Chapter 5: Inhibitors and Failed Reactions 31
Chapter 6: Equilibrium: Sustaining Growth 37
Chapter 7: Implementation Framework: Your Economic Reaction Plan . 43
Chapter 8: The Role of Leadership in Economic Collisions 49
Chapter 9: Community Engagement as Activation Energy 55
Chapter 10: The Role of Technology in Catalyzing Growth 61
Chapter 11: Lessons from Failures 67
Chapter 12: Future Trends in Economic Development 73
Chapter 13: Conclusion: The Future of Economic Collisions 81
Chapter 14: Resources for Practitioners 85

Collision theory states that for a chemical reaction to occur, the reacting particles must collide with one another. The rate of the reaction depends on the frequency of collisions. The theory also tells us that reacting particles often collide without reacting. For collisions to be successful, reacting particles must (1) collide with (2) sufficient energy, and (3) with the proper orientation.

FORWARD

It's not every day that you connect the dots between the world of chemical research and the art of economic development. For most of my career, I've been immersed in the challenges and triumphs of helping communities grow: revitalizing neighborhoods, attracting businesses, and creating environments where people can thrive. But as I worked through these complexities, I found myself repeatedly thinking back to my dad, a physical chemist whose work shaped my childhood and, unknowingly, my professional perspective.

My father, Dr. Gene A. Crowder, spent his career studying the intricacies of chemical reactions, where the collision of molecules under the right conditions could transform matter into something entirely new. He could look at an ordinary interaction in the lab and see its extraordinary potential to spark change. I didn't realize it at the time, but the lessons I absorbed watching him pursue his work, his curiosity, discipline, and ability to connect seemingly unrelated ideas would later form the foundation for my own career.

In chemistry, collision theory explains how particles must collide with sufficient energy and the right orientation for a reaction to occur. It's a straightforward concept, but its implications are profound. Without the right conditions, a collision is just a bump in the dark, yielding no meaningful result. But with the right alignment and energy, that collision can spark a chain reaction, transforming elements, forming new bonds, and unleashing potential.

The more I thought about it, the more I realized that collision theory wasn't just for chemists. It was for community leaders, entrepreneurs, policymakers, and anyone trying to ignite growth and innovation in a complex system. Just as my dad worked tirelessly in his lab to coax reactions into existence, we, as economic developers, must create the conditions for meaningful collisions between people, businesses, and ideas.

This book is about applying the principles of collision theory to economic development. It's about understanding how communities, like chemical systems, are full of potential energy, waiting for the right catalysts to unlock transformative growth. It's about learning from successful reactions and failed experiments, using data, intuition, and ingenuity to guide decisions. And it's about honoring the legacy of a physical chemist whose passion for discovery continues to inspire me. In the following chapters, we'll explore how the dynamics of collision theory can help us think differently about economic development.

We'll look at the elements of a successful reaction: the stakeholders, policies, and resources, as well as the catalysts that can spark action. We'll highlight the barriers preventing change and the lessons we can learn from failed attempts. Along the way, we'll draw on real-world examples, actionable frameworks, and a few stories from my dad's life to make the science of economic growth both relatable and practical. Whether you're a city leader, a business owner, or simply someone invested in your community's future, this book is for you. It's a guide to thinking boldly, creating connections, and igniting growth that transforms places and lives, creating places that people want to be.

Let's get started.

For a free companion Implementation Workbook please visit:
https://businessflare.net/businessflare-publishing-group/

Introduction:
The Chemistry of Economic Growth

"A failed reaction isn't the end. It's just a step toward figuring out what works."

Chemistry was my Dad's life, but it was also his way of seeing the world. He believed that reactions didn't happen by chance; they resulted from understanding the elements involved, creating the right conditions, and applying enough energy to set the process in motion. "A failed reaction isn't the end," he would say. "It's just a step toward figuring out what works."

Growing up, I watched him turn everyday materials into spectacular experiments. His lab was where the ordinary became extraordinary, where he froze bananas to hammer nails, made eggs slip into bottles, and built volcanic eruptions that captured the imagination of everyone around him. He had a way of making science relatable, showing that transformation wasn't just about the materials; it was about understanding the dynamics behind them.

I didn't realize at the time how much those lessons would influence my own work. In my career in economic development, I've found that communities operate like my Dad's chemical systems. They are filled with potential energy: people, businesses, history, and ideas, all waiting for the right conditions to collide and create growth. But potential alone isn't enough. Transformation happens when you create the right conditions, apply the right energy, and keep adapting until you find the formula that works.

Why This Book Matters Now

Communities today are navigating a world that is changing faster than ever. Technology is reshaping industries, demographics are shifting, and economies are becoming more interconnected and unpredictable. The old playbooks for economic development: waiting for outside investment, following rigid plans, or relying on legacy industries, are no longer enough. Communities that thrive in this new era will be the ones that embrace innovation, adaptability, and collaboration.

This book offers a fresh perspective. Drawing on the principles of collision theory, it provides a framework for understanding how communities can unlock their potential and create lasting growth. Instead of looking for solutions from the outside, this approach focuses on exposing, identifying and amplifying the energy, assets, and opportunities that already exist within a community.

What You'll Learn

The Chemistry of Economic Growth is divided into three main sections, each corresponding to a key principle of collision theory:

Activation Energy: This section explores how to overcome inertia and make progress. You'll learn to identify barriers, create momentum, and generate the energy needed to spark local economic growth.

Catalysts and Collisions: Catalysts amplify energy and create transformative change. These chapters focus on finding and nurturing catalysts, aligning stakeholders, and fostering the connections that lead to successful collisions.

Equilibrium and Sustainability: Growth isn't about constant acceleration; it's about finding balance. This section covers strategies for maintaining progress, adapting to change, and creating systems that thrive over time.

The chapters include real-world examples, practical tools, and lessons from my Dad's lab and my community experiences that led to and refined the BusinessFlare® Approach. Whether you're a community leader, a business owner, or simply someone who cares about the future of your town, this book is designed to inspire action and provide you with actionable steps to create meaningful change.

The Power of Connection

At its heart, this book is about connection. Just as molecules must collide with the right energy and alignment to create a reaction, communities must bring people, businesses, and ideas together in ways that spark transformation. But these collisions don't happen by accident. They require leadership, vision, and a willingness to experiment.

I've seen the power of connection firsthand. In one city, a struggling downtown found new life after a few small grants helped local entrepreneurs open storefronts. Those businesses drew foot traffic, inspired others to invest, and turned a stagnant district into a vibrant hub. In another community, a grassroots movement to improve public spaces created new parks, pride, and trust among residents. These moments weren't just about individual projects; they were about creating the conditions where energy could flow and growth could flourish.

A Call to Action

Local economic development isn't about following a set formula; it's about understanding your community's unique dynamics and creating the conditions for transformation. This book isn't just a guide, it's an invitation to see your community through a new lens that values creativity, connection, and the courage to experiment.

As you read, I encourage you to reflect on your community's potential. What energy is waiting to be unlocked? What catalysts are ready to spark change? And what will it take to create the collisions that drive growth? Together, we'll explore how chemistry principles can help you shape a future filled with possibility.

Chapter 1: A Chemist's Legacy

In my Dad's lab, there was always an element of wonder. He had a way of turning the abstract world of molecules and reactions into something vivid and tangible. One of his favorite demonstrations involved building and erupting a volcano. It wasn't a small model, either; it was the kind that could fill a room with excitement. Using baking soda, vinegar, and a mix of other ingredients, he'd recreate the force of nature in a way that left his students and audiences amazed.

The volcano wasn't just a spectacle. It was a lesson in how the right combination of elements, brought together under the right conditions, could create something transformative. My Dad would stand by the model and explain that what they witnessed wasn't magic but chemistry, art, and science of transformation. This same excitement for discovery shaped the way I approach economic development. Just as he saw infinite possibilities in his lab, I see them in communities.

When I started working in economic development, I unknowingly drew on my Dad's lessons more than I expected. Communities, like chemical systems, are filled with potential energy. The challenge is finding ways to release that energy in ways that create growth and opportunity. My Dad's work with reactions, catalysts, and equilibrium became a lens through which I could understand the complexities of economic systems.

Take the volcano, for example. The reaction depended on precise measurements of each ingredient. Too much or too little, and the eruption wouldn't happen. The same is true for economic development. A thriving downtown or industrial district doesn't always emerge by accident. It takes careful planning, strategic investment, and a deep understanding of the conditions that drive success. Understand, that there is no rule about who creates this collision; it isn't always the public sector that does the careful planning, often it's a pioneering entrepreneur that sees potential in an area everyone else has written off.

This book is about applying the principles of collision theory to economic development. It's about understanding how activation energy, catalysts, and alignment can create the conditions for meaningful collisions: moments where people, businesses, and ideas come together to create something greater than the sum of their parts. These principles aren't just theoretical. They are grounded in the lessons I learned from my Dad's work and the real-world challenges I've faced in the communities I've worked in.

The BusinessFlare® Approach is built on the idea that every community has unique strengths waiting to be unlocked if they have the will to improve. Just as my Dad tailored each experiment to the materials and conditions at hand, we must design strategies and tactics that fit a place's specific dynamics. This means listening to residents, engaging stakeholders, and combining data with intuition and instinct to create practical and inspiring actions.

In the following chapters, we'll explore the elements of successful economic reactions. We'll look at how activation energy overcomes inertia, how catalysts amplify progress, and how alignment creates the conditions for sustained growth. Along the way, I'll share stories from my Dad's lab and the communities I've worked with, showing how these principles come to life in scientific and human ways.

As we begin this journey, I want to leave you with the image of that erupting volcano. It reminds us that transformation is about the ingredients and the conditions that bring them together. It's about energy, timing, and creativity. Most of all, it's about believing in the potential of what can be built, whether in a lab or a community.

Exercise: Discovering Your Community's Unique Reaction

Reflect on what makes your community unique. List three characteristics that differentiate it from neighboring areas (e.g., historical assets, industries, cultural traditions).

Identify one challenge that your community faces. How could this challenge be turned into an opportunity?

Kevin S. Crowder

Chapter 2:
Activation Energy:
Overcoming Barriers to Progress

In my Dad's lab, progress wasn't automatic. Even when the ingredients were perfectly measured, and the setup looked flawless, some reactions simply wouldn't happen. It wasn't about the tools or the chemistry itself but about energy. He explained that without activation energy, nothing starts. Activation energy, as he described it, is the push a system needs to overcome inertia and set change in motion.

I didn't realize it then, but that concept would follow me into my work in economic development. Like chemical systems, communities often find themselves at a standstill, filled with potential but lacking the momentum to move forward. Breaking through requires energy in the form of investment, leadership, and/or public enthusiasm, so that you can spark a chain reaction.

The Egg in a Bottle: Creating the Push

One of my Dad's favorite demonstrations was getting an egg into a bottle. The audience would look at the setup, confused about how it could work. The neck of the bottle was far too small for the egg to pass through. But he knew creating the right conditions would make the impossible seem easy. Lighting a piece of paper inside the bottle created a vacuum that pulled the egg through, causing audible gasps from the crowd. "It's all about the push," he would say. "You can't force the egg. You create the energy, and the system takes over."

That story stuck with me because I've seen so many communities in the same position as that egg: filled with potential but blocked by barriers. They need energy to create movement and overcome the inertia that keeps them stuck. This activation energy can take many forms in economic development: a bold investment, a grassroots effort, or a leadership decision that rallies people toward a common goal.

Breaking Through Inertia

I worked with a Florida town stuck in just such a cycle. Its downtown was picturesque but lifeless, its businesses struggling to survive. Local leaders had tried beautification projects and marketing campaigns, but nothing seemed to stick. When I sat down with stakeholders to understand the problem, it became clear that the town lacked a vision and the will to see it through. Each effort was disconnected, creating wasted energy that was never focused.

The breakthrough came when we identified a shared goal: turning downtown into a hub for local art and culture. Now, this is easier said than done, and "arts and culture" can often be the fallback for communities that don't have any other ideas. To be successful, there has to be a focus on authenticity and a willingness to engage in a respectful reality check.

Once the landscape of the art scene was truly understood, feasibility was defined. The town launched a small grant program for local artists and artisans to set up temporary exhibits and workshops in vacant storefronts. This was their activation energy. The program wasn't expensive, but it was enough to bring people downtown and create excitement. The presence of art and activity turned the area into a destination, drawing visitors and inspiring nearby businesses to invest in their spaces.

The BusinessFlare® Approach emphasizes the importance of truly identifying, understanding, and addressing barriers before progress can occur. In many communities, these barriers aren't physical but psychological. Fear of failure, resistance to change, and mistrust among stakeholders can act as potent inhibitors, keeping a community stuck in place. Activation energy breaks through these barriers, creating conditions where people, businesses, and ideas can collide.

Learning from Failure
My Dad's experiments didn't always work perfectly, and community efforts also sometimes fall short. In his lab, the egg would stubbornly refuse to move if the paper didn't burn evenly or the vacuum wasn't strong enough. He didn't give up. He adjusted the setup, tried again, and learned from the failure. This persistence taught me that activation energy isn't just about a single burst of effort. It's about pushing forward, even when the first attempt falls short.

Communities, too, must embrace this mindset. One city I worked with faced years of gridlock over how to redevelop its waterfront. Every proposal stalled as different groups debated priorities. It wasn't until the city launched a tactical pilot project, in the form of a temporary pedestrian plaza, that things began to change. The project wasn't perfect, but it showed what was possible. The plaza became a space where residents and visitors could engage with one another, sparking momentum and the will to pursue larger changes.

Actionable Steps for Activation Energy

Identify Barriers:
Conduct a thorough assessment of what's holding your community back. Are the barriers physical, financial, or psychological? Understanding the root cause is the first step to overcoming it.

Start Small:
Look for initiatives that require minimal resources but can create visible results, such as pop-up shops or pilot projects.

Build Confidence:
Focus on small wins that inspire confidence and show what's possible. Use these wins to generate momentum for larger initiatives.

Engage Stakeholders:
Involve residents, businesses, and community leaders to build trust and ensure buy-in.

Embrace Resilience:
Treat setbacks as opportunities to learn and refine your approach. Keep pushing forward until the conditions are right.

The lesson of activation energy is simple: transformation doesn't happen by accident. It happens because someone creates the conditions where energy can flow, barriers can break, and progress can begin.

Whether it's lighting a match in a bottle or a bold new economic development initiative, the spark makes all the difference.

Exercise: Identifying and Generating Activation Energy

List three barriers that are holding your community back. Consider structural, cultural, or economic factors.

Brainstorm two small-scale initiatives that could serve as activation energy for overcoming these barriers. Who would need to be involved in making these initiatives successful?

Kevin S. Crowder

Chapter 3:
Catalysts: Igniting Economic Growth

"Sometimes the smallest things cause the biggest problems."

Catalysts were my Dad's favorite part of chemistry. He enjoyed explaining how a catalyst could take something ordinary and unlock its extraordinary potential. One of my favorite demonstrations as a kid was the Banana Nail experiment. He would freeze a banana using liquid nitrogen until it became as hard as steel. Then, with a theatrical flair, he'd drive a nail into a block of wood using the frozen banana as a hammer.

The kids were always amazed, but my Dad never let the moment pass without sharing the lesson. "The banana didn't change," he would explain. "It's still a banana. But with the right conditions, it can do something you'd never expect."

This principle resonates deeply in economic development. Communities are full of potential, much like that banana. What they often lack is the catalyst that unlocks and amplifies their energy. A catalyst doesn't create change on its own. It works with what's already there, accelerating progress and making connections that might not have happened otherwise.

How Catalysts Work

In chemistry, catalysts lower the activation energy needed for a reaction, speeding up the process without being consumed. In communities, catalysts serve the same purpose. They reduce barriers, create momentum, and inspire action. Catalysts can take many forms: a visionary leader, a targeted grant program, a grassroots event, a public-private partnership, or even an Instagram post.

The key to a successful catalyst is alignment. Just as a catalyst in the wrong reaction won't work, an economic catalyst must fit the unique dynamics of the community. My Dad used to say, "A good catalyst doesn't force the reaction; it's organic, even in physical chemistry. It just lets it happen." Think about how true this is in those places that we all point to as the best examples of revitalization; if you've read my other writings, you know that this is precisely what led to the resurgence of South Beach in the mid-1980s.

Case Study: The Façade Improvement Grant Program

One of the clearest examples of a successful catalyst comes from many cities we worked with that struggled to revitalize their downtowns. The districts remained stagnant despite having historic architecture, centralized locations, and dedicated business owners. The turning point often came when the city introduced a façade improvement grant program.

The grants offered matching funds to help businesses update their storefronts. The changes seemed small, comprised of fresh paint, new signage, and updated lighting, but the impact was transformative. The updated storefronts attracted more foot traffic, which inspired neighboring businesses to make improvements as well. Within a year, some of these districts had renewed energy, with new businesses opening their doors.

The program didn't just beautify the downtown; it signaled to the community that change was happening. This small intervention acted as a catalyst, amplifying existing assets and creating a ripple effect of growth.

Learning from Missteps

Not every catalyst works as intended. My Dad would say that catalysts aren't magic; they require the conditions to succeed. A state-of-the-art performing arts center was built to anchor a downtown revitalization effort in one city. The building was stunning, but it failed to connect with the community. Residents found it too expensive and formal, while visitors came only for performances and left immediately afterward. Despite its grandeur, the arts center didn't act as a catalyst because it wasn't aligned with the community's needs or identity.

Contrast this with a small rural town that embraced its agricultural heritage. The town created a farm-to-table festival that brought together local farmers, chefs, and artisans. The festival wasn't just an event; t became a celebration of the town's culture. Farmers gained new customers, chefs developed partnerships with local suppliers, and the community found a renewed sense of community pride. What started as a single festival evolved into a movement that strengthened the local economy and preserved the town's character.

Emerging Catalysts in Unexpected Places

Catalysts don't always come from large-scale projects or government programs. Some of the most effective ones emerge from individuals, entrepreneurs, or small initiatives. I worked with a community where a single café owner sparked a downtown revival. She started by hosting live music on Friday nights, turning her café into a gathering place. The energy she created spilled over into neighboring businesses, inspiring them to organize their events. What began as a small effort became the foundation for a broader revitalization effort.

This mirrors the lesson of my Dad's Banana Nail experiment. The banana itself didn't change; rather, it was the conditions created by the liquid nitrogen that allowed it to do something extraordinary. Similarly, communities don't need to change who they are to succeed. They need to find the right conditions to unlock their potential.

Leadership as a Catalyst

Leadership is often the most powerful catalyst. In every successful project I've been part of, a leader has seen an opportunity and acted on it. These leaders, whether mayors, business owners, or engaged residents, inspire others to join in and create the critical mass needed for change. At the end of the day, it is leadership's will that determines success or failure. You can do everything right, but if the council or administration get cold feet or scared, the right conditions evaporate and nothing happens.

In one city, a downtown association director spearheaded the transformation of an underused parking lot into a vibrant outdoor market. The project faced initial skepticism, but her persistence and vision united stakeholders. The market became popular, proving the area could thrive and inspire further investments. In Miami Beach, I saw many examples of strong leadership that catalyzed great projects, such as the Beachwalk and Soundscape Park at the New World Center, the new home of the New World Symphony. I also saw the city commission cave in and lose their will when we had the chance to create a permanent year-round Cirque Du Soleil venue. The city commission's denial of a strong leadership catalyst cost the city a great new entertainment destination and a positive fiscal impact of over $100 million on the city's budget over 10 years.

Actionable Steps for Identifying Catalysts

Understand Your Community's Dynamics: A good catalyst aligns with the community's strengths and values. Start by identifying what makes your community unique.

Start Small: Look for opportunities to test ideas through pilot projects or temporary initiatives. These efforts provide valuable feedback and bui d momentum.

Build Trust: A catalyst is more effective when stakeholders feel invested in its success. Engage the community early and often to ensure buy-in. Leverage Existing Assets: Catalysts don't need to create something new, they amplify what already exists. Focus on enhancing the resources and relationships already present in your community.

The lesson of catalysts is simple: small interventions can lead to big transformations when aligned with a community's identity and energy. Just as my Dad's Banana Nail experiment showed how the right conditions could unlock extraordinary potential, the right catalyst can take a community's assets and turn them into something truly transformative.

Exercise: Finding Catalysts in Your Community

Identify three existing assets or initiatives in your community that could serve as catalysts for growth (e.g., a local leader, an emerging industry, or a successful event).

For each, write a short plan describing how you could amplify its impact. What resources or partnerships would be needed?

Chapter 4:
The Dynamics of Successful Collisions

"Alignment is everything. Without it, all you've got is chaos."

In my Dad's laboratory, nothing happened by chance. He would carefully measure every ingredient, adjust the temperature, and monitor the pressure. But even with the perfect setup, a reaction wouldn't occur unless the molecules collided at just the right angle. "Alignment is everything," he would say. "Without it, all you've got is chaos." Watching him work taught me that successful reactions depend on energy and precision, that is, the careful orchestration of elements to create something transformative.

The Role of Alignment in Success

Communities, like chemical systems, are made up of moving parts. People, businesses, and ideas constantly interact, but not all interactions lead to progress. For meaningful growth to occur, these elements need to collide in aligned, intentional, and energized ways. Alignment ensures that efforts are not wasted, and energy ensures that those efforts have momentum.

I once worked with a mid-sized city struggling to revitalize its downtown. Despite having a rich history, a central location, and strong civic pride, the district remained stagnant. The problem wasn't a lack of energy; there were plenty of ideas and initiatives. Too many in fact. The issue was alignment. Stakeholders were working at cross-purposes. Local businesses wanted to attract residents, while city leaders were focused on drawing in tourists. This misalignment meant that resources were spread thin, and efforts failed to create lasting change.

The breakthrough came when we brought all the stakeholders together to develop a shared and realistic vision. By aligning their goals, they could focus their energy on a single initiative: transforming an underused plaza into a community gathering space. This project created a place where residents and visitors could connect (and collide), sparking new energy for the district. The plaza became the starting point for a broader revitalization effort, showing that alignment is the foundation of successful collisions.

The Power of Energy and Momentum

Energy is the other critical ingredient in successful collisions. In chemistry, molecules need enough energy to break old bonds and form new ones. In communities, energy comes from leadership, investment, and public enthusiasm. It's what turns ideas into action and potential into progress.

One city demonstrated the power of energy through a series of pop-up events in its struggling downtown. These events, ranging from food festivals to outdoor yoga classes, created a sense of excitement and drew people into the area. The energy generated by these gatherings inspired local entrepreneurs to open new businesses, knowing they could count on foot traffic and community support. Over time, the pop-ups evolved into permanent features, transforming the downtown into a lively destination.

Momentum sustains progress once it begins. My Dad used to explain that once a chemical reaction starts, it often sustains itself, with each collision creating the energy needed for the next. This is called Critical Mass. In communities, momentum works the same way. A single success can inspire confidence, attract investment, and create a chain reaction of growth.

In one rural town, a small bookstore catalyzed a downtown revival. The bookstore attracted customers who then explored nearby shops and cafés. Seeing the increased activity, other entrepreneurs began investing in the area. The momentum built gradually but became self-sustaining as more people were drawn to the district. In economic development, we call it reaching Critical Mass when a business district starts organically attracting new businesses, building upon itself and its success.

Learning from Failure

Not all collisions are successful. My Dad's experiments often included reactions that didn't work out, and the same is true for communities. Some collisions fail because the energy isn't there, and others fail because the pieces aren't aligned. These failures can be frustrating, but they are also valuable. Each setback offers lessons that can guide future efforts.

Communities that embrace a mindset of seeing failure as part of the process are better positioned to adapt and innovate. I once worked with a city that had tried multiple revitalization strategies, only to see them fall short. Instead of giving up, the city's leaders reviewed what went wrong and adjusted. They discovered that their earlier efforts had focused too heavily on attracting visitors without considering the needs of residents and local employees. By shifting their approach to prioritize mixed-use development, quality of life, and local amenities, they created a more sustainable model for growth.

Actionable Steps for Successful Collisions

Foster Alignment:
Bring stakeholders together to develop a shared vision and align goals. Use facilitated workshops or strategic planning sessions to identify common priorities.

Generate Energy:
Focus on initiatives that create excitement and draw people together, such as pop-up events or pilot projects.
Leverage leadership and public enthusiasm to sustain momentum.

Build Momentum:
Start with small, visible wins to inspire confidence and attract further investment.
Track progress and celebrate successes to maintain engagement.

Learn from Setbacks:
Treat failures as opportunities to refine strategies and build resilience.
Engage stakeholders in reviewing what went wrong and adjust plans accordingly.

Exercise: Aligning Goals for Meaningful Collisions

Think about a recent community initiative. Were the stakeholders aligned in their goals? If not, what were the points of misalignment?

Write a strategy for bringing those stakeholders together. What common goals or values could serve as a foundation for alignment?

Kevin S. Crowder

Chapter 5:
Inhibitors and Failed Reactions

"An inhibitor doesn't just stop the reaction; It stops the potential."

In chemistry, inhibitors are the hidden culprits that can derail even the most promising experiments. My Dad often lamented how a reaction that seemed perfect on paper could fail because of an invisible contaminant. These substances slow down or block reactions, preventing molecules from colliding effectively. "An inhibitor doesn't just stop the reaction," he'd say. "It stops the potential."

Communities face their own inhibitors, the forces that block growth, stifle creativity, or prevent connections from happening. These barriers might be structural, like outdated infrastructure or restrictive policies, or cultural, like mistrust, elitism, or fear of change. Identifying and addressing these inhibitors is critical because they act as roadblocks to progress.

Recognizing Inhibitors

In one of his experiments, Dad worked tirelessly to create a specific compound but kept hitting a wall. He tried adjusting the temperature, increasing the pressure, and tweaking the formula, but nothing worked. Frustrated, he finally discovered the problem: a tiny impurity in his materials was blocking the reaction. Once he isolated and removed the contaminant, the reaction occurred immediately. "Sometimes the smallest things cause the biggest problems," he told me.

The same principle applies to communities. Inhibitors can take many forms, but they often thrive in spaces where people are most comfortable. Fear of failure, resistance to change, or entrenched power dynamics are powerful barriers to innovation, adaptation, and success. These inhibitors aren't always visible, but their impact is profound. Addressing them requires careful observation, honest dialogue, and a willingness to confront uncomfortable truths. Essentially, a respectful reality check.

Case Study: The Paralysis of Fear

I've already mentioned that I worked with a small town that had spent decades trying to revitalize its downtown. On paper, the town had everything it needed: historic architecture, a strong sense of community, and dedicated leaders. What we call "strong bones" in a way overused way. Yet every proposal for change was met with resistance. Residents feared revitalization would erase the town's identity and create negative phantom impacts, while business owners worried about the risks of investing in uncertain times. This fear created a paralysis that kept the town stuck in place.

The breakthrough came when we shifted the focus from large-scale change to incremental wins. Instead of proposing sweeping redevelopment, we started with temporary initiatives like outdoor markets and pop-up shops. Places for people to engage with one another. These small projects showed residents that progress didn't have to come at the expense of the town's character. Over time, the fear subsided, and larger changes became possible, all within the context of community character.

The Cost of Misalignment

Another common inhibitor is misalignment among stakeholders. A redevelopment project stalled for years in one city because leaders and developers couldn't agree on priorities. City officials wanted to prioritize affordable housing, while developers focused on maximizing profits with high-end commercial space. This lack of alignment created delays, cost overruns, and a growing sense of frustration, all in the context of changing market dynamics and the financing environment.

The turning point came when both sides sat down to identify shared goals. By finding common ground, such as incorporating a mix of housing types and retail options, they were able to move forward. The project didn't just solve a practical problem; it also restored trust and collaboration among stakeholders.

Cultural Inhibitors

Some inhibitors are deeply embedded in a community's identity. Fear of change is one of the most persistent. In one rural town, leaders hesitated to embrace tourism as an economic strategy because they worried it would disrupt their way of life. While their concerns were valid, their resistance kept the town from exploring opportunities that could have revitalized its economy.

The solution wasn't to dismiss their fears but to address them directly. Leaders shifted the narrative by framing tourism as a way to celebrate and preserve the town's heritage. This approach allowed the community to move forward without losing its identity.

Actionable Steps for Addressing Inhibitors

Identify the Root Cause:
Conduct a thorough assessment to uncover the barriers holding your community back. Are they structural, cultural, elitist, or psychological?

Foster Open Dialogue:
Create spaces where stakeholders can voice their concerns and share their perspectives. Honest conversations are key to identifying inhibitors.

Start with Small Wins:
Focus on achievable projects that build trust and demonstrate progress. These wins can help overcome fear and resistance.

Align Priorities:
Bring stakeholders together to identify shared goals and create a unified vision. Misalignment wastes energy and stalls progress.

Embrace Adaptability:
Be willing to adjust strategies based on feedback and changing conditions. Flexibility is essential for overcoming barriers.

Learning from Failure

My Dad used to say that failed experiments weren't wasted but rather lessons in disguise. Each time a reaction didn't work, he learned something new about the system he was working with. Communities, too, can learn from setbacks. Failed projects reveal what doesn't work, providing valuable insights for future efforts.

One city I worked with launched a business incubator to attract startups to its downtown. The program failed to gain traction because it didn't address the needs of the local ecosystem. Instead of abandoning the idea, the city retooled the program to focus on supporting existing small businesses. This shift in strategy led to a more sustainable and impactful initiative.

Exercise: Diagnosing and Overcoming Inhibitors

Reflect on a time when a project or initiative in your community failed to gain traction. What were the inhibitors that blocked progress?

Develop a plan for addressing one of these inhibitors. What steps could you take to remove it and create the conditions for success?

Kevin S. Crowder

Chapter 6:
Equilibrium: Sustaining Growth

In chemistry, equilibrium is the point where a reaction reaches balance. Dad explained it as the moment when the forward and reverse reactions occur simultaneously, creating a state of stability. It wasn't about stopping the reaction but finding a rhythm where the system could sustain itself. This concept has stuck with me because it mirrors what communities must achieve for long-term success.

Sustaining growth requires balance. Communities cannot endlessly push for more development or afford to become complacent. They must find a way to grow harmoniously with their identity, resources, and long-term goals. Achieving equilibrium means creating systems that adapt to change without losing their core values. It also means you don't have to just listen to the preachy planners tell you what they think is best; find your equilibrium on your terms.

The Balance of Progress and Preservation
One of the best examples of equilibrium in action comes from a coastal town that embraced sustainable tourism. For years, the town relied

on seasonal visitors for its beaches and fishing charters. While tourism brought in revenue, it also created challenges, from overcrowding to environmental degradation. Local leaders realized they couldn't keep growing without addressing these issues. They worked with residents and businesses to create a tourism management plan that balanced economic benefits with environmental and community health. Managing the number of visitors during peak seasons and investing in eco-friendly infrastructure, the town found a way to sustain its growth without sacrificing its character.

This balance is not static. Dad used to say that equilibrium wasn't the absence of change but the ability to maintain balance through change. This means staying flexible and responsive to new challenges and opportunities in communities.

It also means recognizing when adjustments are needed to avoid tipping too far in one direction. For most cities, this is the hardest part: not the recognition itself that adjustments are needed, but the will to make the adjustments.

Adjusting to Maintain Stability

In one city we worked with, a successful downtown revitalization effort began to create unintended consequences as new businesses and residents moved in, and rising property values threatened to displace long-time residents and small businesses. Local leaders addressed this imbalance by creating programs to support affordable housing and small business retention. These actions allowed the community to sustain its momentum while preserving its unique character.

This principle aligns closely with the BusinessFlare® Approach, which emphasizes balancing growth with economic and community sustainability. This is where the philosophy described in "Gut Sandwich" becomes especially important. Data can show us where growth is happening, but intuition and storytelling help us understand the deeper dynamics at play and to trust our gut.

Equilibrium and Community Identity

Achieving equilibrium also requires a clear understanding of a community's identity. Dad often said that every chemical reaction had its own personality, shaped by the unique properties of its elements. The same is true for communities. Growth that aligns with a community's identity is far more sustainable than growth that feels imposed or disconnected. For example, a small town known for its agricultural heritage might thrive by building on that identity through farm-to-table initiatives or agri-tourism. By staying true to its roots, the town can grow in an authentic and lasting way.

Leadership and Long-Term Vision

Leadership plays a crucial role in maintaining equilibrium. Effective leaders understand that their role isn't just to drive and guide growth. They listen to their communities, anticipate challenges, and make decisions that balance short-term gains with long-term stability. In every community I've worked with, the most successful leaders have been those who could see the bigger picture, balancing competing priorities without losing sight of the community's core values.

Actionable Steps for Achieving Equilibrium

Define Core Values:
Identify what makes your community unique and use it as the foundation for growth strategies.

Monitor and Adjust:
Regularly evaluate the impact of growth initiatives and make adjustments to maintain balance.

Engage Stakeholders:
Involve residents, businesses, and leaders in decision-making to ensure that diverse perspectives are considered.

Plan for Sustainability:
Invest in programs and infrastructure that support long-term stability, such as affordable housing, workforce development, or environmental initiatives.

Balance Data and Intuition:
Use measurable insights to guide decisions while considering the values and stories that define your community.

Equilibrium is not a Destination

It's an ongoing process of learning, adapting, and recalibrating. Communities that embrace this mindset are better equipped to handle uncertainty and change. They recognize that progress is not about reaching a fixed endpoint but creating systems that sustain growth over time.

Exercise: Balancing Growth and Sustainability

Identify two areas where your community is thriving and two areas where it is struggling. How might the thriving areas help support the struggling ones to create balance?

Write a short vision statement that describes what equilibrium would look like in your community.

Kevin S. Crowder

Chapter 7:
Implementation Framework:
Your Economic Reaction Plan

"A good experiment isn't rigid, it's a process of learning and refining."

My Dad's lab was a place of constant curiosity and experimentation, and I loved visiting it and roaming the halls of the West Texas State Science Center and all of the departments. I especially liked to go see the snakes in the Biology Department. He approached every reaction with a plan but also knew the importance of adapting as new variables came into play. "A good experiment isn't rigid," he'd say. "It's a process of learning and refining." This mindset is just as essential in economic development as chemistry. Communities don't transform by chance.

They transform when leaders, stakeholders, and residents collaborate to design and implement a plan aligning resources, energy, and goals. This chapter provides an actionable framework for communities to apply the principles of collision theory and the BusinessFlare® Approach. It's not just about strategy; it's about creating the conditions where progress can thrive and sustain itself.

Step 1: Assess Your Community's Dynamics

Every reaction begins with an understanding of the materials at hand. My Dad always started his experiments by analyzing the properties of the elements he worked with. This means taking stock of your assets, challenges, and opportunities in communities.

Understand Your Strengths: What makes your community unique? This could be its location, history, industries, or cultural assets.

Identify Barriers: What's holding your community back? Are there structural, financial, or psychological inhibitors that must be addressed?

Engage Stakeholders: Who are your community's key players? This includes residents, business owners, government leaders, and other partners.

Tools like BusinessFlare's Street Economics™ can provide valuable insights into demographics, foot traffic, and real estate trends. But equally important are the stories and instincts of the people who live and work in the community. Data provides a foundation, but intuition and lived experience fill in the gaps.

Step 2: Define Your Vision

A clear vision serves as the guiding star for any economic reaction plan. Without it, energy and resources can become scattered, leading to frustration and wasted effort.

Be Specific: Your vision should be ambitious but actionable. For example, a city might aim to become a regional hub for the arts or a leader in green innovation.

Unify Stakeholders: Use your vision to align goals and create buy-in from diverse groups. This prevents misalignment and ensures that everyone is working toward the same outcome.

Communicate Clearly: A compelling vision resonates with both data and emotion. Share your vision in a way that inspires action and fosters trust.

Step 3: Design Your Catalysts

Catalysts accelerate progress by amplifying existing energy. My Dad would experiment with different catalysts to see which produced the best results. In communities, catalysts can take many forms, from targeted investments to grassroots initiatives.

Start Small: Pilot projects or temporary programs can provide proof of concept while minimizing risk.

Leverage Existing Assets: Catalysts don't need to create something new; they amplify what already exists. Focus on enhancing your community's unique strengths. This is the foundation of the BusinessFlare® Approach, more specifically, identifying your "Expose" opportunities. Learn more about this approach in "Governing for Economic Development" and "Gut Sandwich."

Ensure Alignment: A catalyst works best when it aligns with your community's place brand and goals. Avoid imposing solutions that feel disconnected or forced. One example comes from a city that used a grant program to support local entrepreneurs. By helping a few pioneering businesses open storefronts, the program created a ripple effect of investment and activity that transformed the downtown district.

Step 4: Implement with Precision

Implementation is where your plan becomes reality. This phase requires leadership, collaboration, and attention to detail. Dad used to say that a reaction wasn't finished until every variable had been tested and refined. In our communities, this means staying engaged throughout the process and being willing to adapt as needed.

Build Momentum: Focus on visible wins that inspire confidence and attract further investment.

Engage the Community: Involve residents and stakeholders to build trust and ensure buy-in.

Monitor Progress: Use data and feedback to track outcomes and adjust your approach. This keeps the process dynamic and responsive.

Step 5: Measure and Sustain

Every experiment in my Dad's lab ended with meticulous documentation. Even failures were recorded, as they provided valuable insights for future efforts. Measurement is just as critical in economic development.

Track Progress: Set clear but reasonablemetrics for success and regularly evaluate your results.

Celebrate Wins: Highlight milestones to maintain enthusiasm and build momentum.

Plan for Sustainability: Create systems and programs that can adapt to change while preserving your community's core values. One community achieved sustainability by establishing a business improvement district (BID). Local businesses contributed funding for marketing, events, and maintenance, reducing reliance on public resources and ensuring long-term stability.

Actionable Framework Summary

Assess Your Dynamics: Understand your assets, barriers, and stakeholders.

Define Your Vision: Create a unifying goal that aligns and inspires.

Design Your Catalysts: Identify small but strategic interventions to accelerate progress.

Implement with Precision: Focus on visible wins, community engagement, and adaptability.

Measure and Sustain: Track outcomes, celebrate successes, and build systems for the long term.

Communities thrive when the right conditions are in place, like chemical systems. Following this framework can turn potential into progress, creating the energy, alignment, and momentum needed to drive transformation.

Kevin S. Crowder

Chapter 8:
The Role of Leadership in Economic Collisions

In every community I've worked with, leadership has been the deciding factor between inertia and momentum. Dad used to say that a reaction is only as strong as its catalyst, and I can tell you that leaders (public and private sector) often serve as the most powerful catalysts. They bring people together, inspire action, and create the alignment needed for meaningful collisions.

Leadership as a Catalyst

Leadership isn't just about making decisions. It's about creating the conditions where others can thrive. In one struggling downtown, a local business owner took it upon herself to organize a monthly street market. At first, it was a small event, with only a handful of vendors and visitors.

However, her persistence and enthusiasm inspired other businesses to join in, and the market grew into a major draw for the district. She wasn't a city official or a professional planner; she simply saw an opportunity and acted on it.

This kind of grassroots leadership is often the spark that ignites change. Leaders at every level, from local government to neighborhood and business associations, can serve as catalysts by identifying opportunities, rallying support, and setting things in motion.

Traits of Transformative Leaders

Transformative leaders share several key traits that enable them to drive meaningful change:

Vision: They can see the potential in their community and articulate a clear, compelling vision for the future.

Empathy: They listen to diverse perspectives and build trust by addressing the concerns of all stakeholders.

Resilience: They persist in the face of setbacks, using failures as opportunities to learn and adapt.

Collaboration: They bring people together, creating alignment across sectors and interests.

Action-Oriented: They don't wait for perfect conditions; they act decisively to create momentum.

One mayor I worked with exemplified these traits. Her city was facing economic decline, with businesses closing and residents leaving. Instead of focusing on what the city lacked, she focused on its strengths: a vibrant arts community and a growing tourism sector. She championed policies that supported local artists, invested in public art installations, and worked with businesses to create visitor-friendly experiences. Her leadership transformed the city into a cultural destination, attracting new residents and investments.

Balancing Data and Intuition

The best leaders understand the importance of balancing measurable insights with intuition. This is the essence of the Gut Sandwich philosophy. Data can provide a clear picture of where a community stands and what opportunities exist, but intuition and storytelling connect people to the vision.

In one community, data revealed that foot traffic in the downtown core had been declining for years. The numbers indicated a need for revitalization, but the specifics weren't clear. Drawing on her deep knowledge of the area, a local entrepreneur proposed creating a pedestrian plaza to encourage gatherings and events. Her instincts were validated when the project brought new energy and activity to the district, proving that data and intuition work best together.

Actionable Steps for Building Leadership Capacity

Identify Potential Leaders:
Look for individuals who are passionate about their community, whether they are business owners, residents, or officials. Please support them with training, resources, and opportunities to lead.

Foster Collaboration:
Create spaces where leaders from different sectors can connect, share ideas, and build partnerships. Facilitate alignment by helping stakeholders find common goals.

Provide Support:
Offer leadership development programs focusing on communication, conflict resolution, and strategic planning.
Recognize and celebrate the contributions of local leaders to inspire others.

Encourage Risk-Taking:
Create a culture where experimentation and innovation are valued.
Frame failures as learning opportunities rather than setbacks.

Leadership's Role in Sustaining Progress

Leadership doesn't stop once a project is launched. Sustaining growth requires leaders who are committed to long-term success. This means staying engaged, monitoring progress, and adjusting as needed. It also means mentoring the next generation of leaders to ensure continuity and resilience.

In one rural town, a long-time community leader made it her mission to mentor young residents passionate about improving their hometown. By sharing her knowledge and creating opportunities for them to lead, she ensured that the progress she helped spark would continue well into the future.

Leaders are the catalysts that transform potential into progress. They create alignment, inspire action, and build the momentum for meaningful collisions. By investing in leadership capacity and fostering a culture of collaboration and innovation, communities can unlock the full potential of their people and assets.

Exercise: Identifying Transformative Leaders

Prompt: Who are the leaders in your community, formal or informal, who are driving progress? List three individuals or organizations and their contributions.

Follow-Up: What traits make them effective? How can you support or empower them to expand their impact?

Exercise: Leadership Traits Reflection

Prompt: Reflect on your leadership style or that of someone you admire. Which traits of transformative leaders (vision, empathy, resilience, collaboration, action-oriented) are most prominent?

Follow-Up: Which trait could be further developed, and how?

Kevin S. Crowder

Chapter 9: Community Engagement as Activation Energy

In economic development, no initiative succeeds without the support of the people it's meant to serve. My Dad used to say that a reaction needs the right energy to break through inertia, and in communities, that energy often comes from the people themselves. Engagement isn't just a step in the process, it's the force that drives progress and creates momentum for lasting change.

The Power of Community Buy-In

When residents are engaged, they become invested in the success of their community. They bring ideas, energy, and support to projects, turning abstract plans into tangible results. In one small town I worked with, the local government was hesitant to invest in a downtown revitalization plan, fearing it wouldn't gain traction. The turning point came when residents organized a community clean-up day, transforming neglected public spaces into vibrant gathering spots. This grassroots effort demonstrated the community's commitment and convinced local leaders to move forward with the plan.

Engagement isn't just about getting people involved, it's about making them feel heard. When people see their ideas reflected in a project, they are more likely to support it and rally others to join.

Strategies for Effective Engagement

Start with Listening:
Engagement begins with understanding the community's needs, values, and concerns. Surveys, public meetings, and focus groups can provide valuable insights. Listening builds trust and creates a foundation for collaboration.

Use Storytelling to Inspire:
Data alone isn't enough to drive action. Stories connect people emotionally to a project, making them feel part of something bigger. Share stories of similar places that have succeeded, showing what's possible.

Meeting People Where They Are:
Engagement efforts should be accessible and inclusive, and build credibility. This might mean hosting events in familiar locations, using plain language, or providing translation services. Social media and digital tools can also help reach a wider audience.

Case Study: Revitalizing Through Participation

Leaders realized they couldn't succeed without public support in a mid-sized city with a struggling downtown. Instead of starting with a traditional top-down plan, they launched a series of workshops where residents could share their ideas for the district. These sessions revealed a strong desire for more public art and green spaces, which weren't part of the original plan.

Leaders adjusted their approach, incorporating these elements into the revitalization strategy. This improved the plan and created a sense of ownership among residents. When the first public art installation was unveiled, it drew a large crowd, sparking new energy for the project and attracting private investment.

Overcoming Barriers to Engagement

Just as chemical reactions face inhibitors, community engagement efforts can encounter resistance. People may feel disconnected, distrustful, or too busy to participate. Overcoming these barriers requires intentionality and creativity.

Build Trust:
A history of failed projects or broken promises can create skepticism. Rebuilding trust takes time, transparency, and consistent follow-through. Highlight small, visible wins to show that change is possible.

Make It Fun:
Engagement doesn't have to be dry or formal. Festivals, art walks, and interactive workshops can bring people together in ways that feel celebratory rather than obligatory. Gamification, including using contests or rewards, can also motivate participation.

Empower Marginalized Voices:
Ensure that engagement efforts include diverse perspectives, especially from historically underserved groups.

Actionable Steps for Community Engagement

Conduct Listening Sessions:
Host town halls, focus groups, or surveys to gather input and build trust. Use data visualization tools to make complex information accessible and relatable.

Create Opportunities for Collaboration:
Invite residents to co-design projects through participatory planning sessions. encourage partnerships between local organizations, businesses, and residents.

Celebrate Progress:
Use community events to showcase milestones and inspire further participation. Highlight the contributions of individuals and groups to foster a sense of pride.

Adapt Based on Feedback:
Treat engagement as an ongoing process, not a one-time effort. Regularly check in with the community and adjust plans as needed.

The Role of Storytelling in Engagement

My Dad's chemistry demonstrations were as much about storytelling as they were about science. Whether he was freezing a banana or creating a mini-volcano, he captured his audience's attention by connecting them to the process. In the same way, community engagement thrives when people feel connected to the story of their community.

One rural town embraced storytelling as a central part of its tourism strategy. Residents were invited to share personal anecdotes about their favorite local spots, which were then featured in marketing campaigns. This attracted visitors and deepened residents' pride in their town.

Building Energy for Long-Term Change

Engagement isn't just about completing a single project; it's about creating a culture where people feel empowered to shape their community. This culture of engagement generates energy that sustains progress over time.

In one city, a downtown association launched a "Future Leaders" program to involve young people in decision-making. By giving them a voice in the process, the city gained fresh ideas and cultivated the next generation of engaged citizens.

Community engagement is the activation energy that breaks through barriers and sets progress in motion. By involving residents, listening to their needs, and building trust, communities can generate the energy and momentum needed to create meaningful change.

Exercise: Designing Engagement Strategies

Prompt: Think of a current or upcoming initiative in your community. Who needs to be engaged for it to succeed? List key groups or individuals.

Follow-Up: Identify two specific methods (e.g., public forums, surveys, focus groups) you could use to engage these groups.

Exercise: Storytelling for Engagement

Prompt: Write a short narrative explaining why this initiative matters to your community. Include a personal or relatable element to inspire connection.

Follow-Up: How could this story be shared to encourage participation?

Chapter 10:
The Role of Technology in Catalyzing Growth

Technology has transformed how communities grow, connect, and adapt. Just as my Dad used specific tools to control reactions in his lab, technology serves as a tool for amplifying energy and aligning efforts in economic development. It enhances processes, supports decision-making, and creates opportunities but doesn't replace human creativity or intuition.

Technology as a Catalyst for Growth

In my Dad's lab, catalysts amplified the potential already present in a reaction. Similarly, technology amplifies the energy and ideas within a community. It supports existing efforts and accelerates the process of turning vision into action.

In one of our cities we used data analytics to analyze foot traffic patterns in its downtown district. The data revealed high-traffic and underperforming areas, helping city planners identify gaps in connectivity. With this insight, the city focused its revitalization efforts on improving pathways between these areas, adding signage and infrastructure enhancements to guide visitors. This targeted intervention led to a more cohesive and dynamic downtown experience.

Smart Cities and Connected Communities

The concept of smart cities, where technology integrates seamlessly into infrastructure and services, has gained attention in recent years. These systems leverage sensors, data, and automation to improve efficiency and quality of life. While this approach is often associated with major urban centers, small towns can also benefit.

Examples include:
Sensors that monitor traffic flow or air quality provide real-time insights for city planners.

Digital platforms that make public services more accessible and allow residents to report issues.

Energy management systems that reduce costs and environmental impact, such as smart lighting or renewable energy integration.

A mid-sized city introduced smart parking sensors to guide drivers to available spaces in its downtown district. This reduced congestion improved the visitor experience and generated valuable data about parking demand that informed future investments.

Technology in Community Engagement

Digital tools have revolutionized how communities engage with their residents. Platforms like social media, online surveys, and virtual town halls make gathering input, sharing updates, and building consensus easier. Many communities embraced these tools during the pandemic to ensure public engagement could continue when in-person events were limited.

In one community, an interactive map allowed residents to pinpoint areas they felt needed improvement, such as unsafe intersections or neglected parks. The tool became a collaborative platform, fostering dialogue and shaping a shared vision for the future.

Opportunities and Risks of Technology

While technology offers enormous potential, it also brings challenges. Over-reliance on data risks creating decisions that feel disconnected from residents' lived experiences. Privacy concerns and unequal access to digital tools can exacerbate divisions.

The key to successful integration lies in balance. Technology should complement intuition and storytelling, not replace them. Data provides clarity, but the people behind the numbers bring the vision to life. Balancing these elements ensures technology serves the community's needs and values.

Actionable Steps for Leveraging Technology

Assess Your Needs:
Identify specific challenges that technology can address, such as improving access to services or providing better data for decision-making.

Choose Scalable Solutions:
Focus on technologies that align with your community's size, budget, and long-term goals.

Train Your Team:
Provide training to ensure staff and stakeholders can use the tools effectively and confidently.

Combine Data with Local Knowledge:
Use data to guide decisions while incorporating intuition and community feedback to create well-rounded strategies.

Engage the Community:
Involve residents through digital engagement tools, ensuring transparency and inclusivity.

The Future of Technology in Economic Development

The rapid pace of technological innovation shows no signs of slowing. Artificial intelligence, virtual reality, and blockchain are already transforming industries and creating new opportunities. While these advancements may feel abstract or distant, their potential to reshape communities is significant.

One rural town embraced virtual reality to attract visitors during the off-season. The town reached a global audience and inspired future tourism by creating a VR experience showcasing its natural beauty and historic landmarks. This innovative approach proved that even small communities can leverage emerging technologies to address challenges and create opportunities.

Technology is a tool that amplifies energy, fosters alignment and creates new possibilities. Communities that embrace innovation while staying true to their identity can use technology to achieve meaningful and lasting growth. By balancing technology's capabilities with the values and needs of the people it serves, communities can chart a course for a more connected and sustainable future.

Exercise: Identifying Tech Opportunities

Prompt: Think about your community's biggest challenges. How could technology help solve these problems? List three possible applications (e.g., data visualization, engagement platforms, AI-driven tools).

Follow-Up: What partnerships or resources would you need to implement these solutions?

Exercise: Digital Engagement Plan

Prompt: Design a digital engagement strategy for a specific project in your community. Which tools (e.g., social media, virtual town halls, interactive maps) would you use, and why?

Follow-Up: How would you measure the success of your engagement efforts?

Kevin S. Crowder

Chapter 11:
Lessons from Failures:
What Communities Can Learn from Missed Opportunities

"A failure isn't the end; it's just part of the process."

In Dad's lab, failed experiments weren't wasted; they were steps toward understanding. He kept meticulous notes on every attempt, whether it succeeded or not because even failures revealed something valuable. "A failure isn't the end," he would say. "It's just part of the process." This mindset is just as important in economic development as in chemistry. Communities that learn from setbacks are better equipped to adapt, innovate, and thrive.

Failures in economic development often result from misalignment, insufficient energy, overlooked barriers, absurd politics, or poor administration. By studying what went wrong, communities can uncover the lessons that lead to better strategies and stronger outcomes.

Case Study: A Missed Tipping Point

A major redevelopment project stalled in one city because stakeholders couldn't agree on a shared vision. The city council wanted to focus on affordable housing, while developers pushed for high-end retail and luxury condos. This misalignment led to delays, cost overruns, and growing frustration among residents. By the time the project finally moved forward, the market had shifted, and much of the original momentum was lost.

The lesson here is the importance of alignment. Successful collisions require stakeholders to work together toward a common goal. When priorities clash, energy dissipates, and opportunities slip away. Communities must invest time building consensus and ensuring that all voices are heard before moving forward.

The Consequences of Ignoring Barriers

Another community I worked with launched a business incubator downtown, hoping to attract startups and revitalize the area. The program offered office space, mentorship, and networking opportunities but failed to gain traction. Many startups left within months, citing a lack of skilled workers and limited local customers. The initiative, while well-intentioned, didn't address the deeper barriers preventing growth.

This failure highlights the importance of understanding a community's dynamics before acting. Economic development efforts must consider the underlying conditions that shape success. Addressing barriers like workforce development, infrastructure gaps, or public perception is often the first step toward meaningful progress.

What Failed Experiments Teach Us

My Dad's experiments often faced setbacks because of inhibitors, contaminants, or external factors that disrupted the reaction. When a reaction failed, he didn't discard the materials. Instead, he analyzed the set-up, identified the problem, and adjusted his approach. Communities can follow the same process when faced with failure:

Analyze the Outcome: What went wrong, and why? Was it a lack of energy, alignment, or resources? Understanding the root cause is critical. Gather Feedback: Talk to stakeholders to learn what they experienced and how the process could improve. Listening builds trust and provides valuable insights.

Adjust the Strategy: Use what you've learned to refine your approach. Failure isn't a reason to stop; it's a reason to adapt.

The Role of Resilience

Resilience is the ability to bounce back from setbacks, and it's one of the most valuable traits a community can cultivate. A series of failed grant applications in one small town nearly derailed plans to restore a historic theater. Instead of giving up, local leaders worked with residents to crowdfund the initial renovations, proving that the project was viable. The theater eventually secured additional funding and became a cornerstone of the downtown district.

Failures are inevitable, but communities that embrace resilience can turn setbacks into stepping stones. This requires a mindset that values persistence, creativity, and collaboration.

Actionable Steps for Learning from Failures

Document the Process:
Keep detailed records of initiatives, including what worked and what didn't. This creates a foundation for learning and improvement.

Conduct Post-Mortems (After Actions):
After a project concludes, gather stakeholders to review the outcomes and identify lessons learned. Focus on constructive feedback rather than assigning blame.

Engage the Community:
To build transparency and trust, share both successes and failures with residents. Highlight how setbacks will inform future efforts.

Adjust and Experiment:
Treat failure as an opportunity to test new ideas. Small pilot projects can provide valuable insights without committing significant resources.

Turning Setbacks into Success

One of the most powerful lessons my Dad taught me was that failure isn't final. It's an opportunity to learn, adapt, and grow. In economic development, the same principle applies. Communities that analyze their failures, engage their stakeholders, and remain committed to progress are the ones that ultimately succeed.

Failures are not roadblocks; they are stepping stones to understanding. By embracing this mindset, communities can unlock new opportunities, build resilience, and create the conditions for lasting growth.

Exercise: Learning from Past Setbacks

Prompt: Think of a failed project or initiative in your community. List the factors contributing to its failure (e.g., misalignment, insufficient energy, lack of resources).

Follow-Up: What steps could have prevented or addressed these inhibitors? Write a brief "what we learned" summary.

Exercise: Building Resilience

Prompt: Identify a current challenge in your community. How can you approach it with resilience and adaptability?

Follow-Up: List two potential alternative strategies if the first approach doesn't succeed.

Kevin S. Crowder

Chapter 12:
Future Trends in Economic Development: Adapting to What's Next

Economic development is about transformation, and change has never been faster. Communities that anticipate emerging trends and adapt strategically will position themselves as leaders in the years to come. Technological shifts, workforce dynamics, and the evolving relationship between place and people drive these trends.

This chapter explores the trends shaping the next decade of economic development and provides actionable strategies for communities to remain competitive, relevant, and vibrant.

Remote Work and Distributed Economies

The rise of remote work is reshaping where and how people live and work. This shift creates opportunities for communities to attract talent and investment by offering the right mix of infrastructure and lifestyle amenities.

Opportunities:
Smaller cities and towns can compete with major urban centers by emphasizing affordability, livability, and digital connectivity.

Co-working spaces and "work-from-anywhere" initiatives can establish local hubs of economic activity.

Strategies for Communities:
Develop high-speed internet infrastructure to attract remote workers.

Create co-working spaces, flexible office hubs, and networking events for remote professionals.

Promote your community as a haven for digital nomads and remote workers through targeted marketing campaigns.

Digital Economies and Entrepreneurship

The rise of e-commerce and digital platforms is democratizing market access, enabling businesses of all sizes to reach customers globally.

Communities that foster entrepreneurship can benefit from this economic transformation.

Opportunities:
Local entrepreneurs can use digital platforms to expand their reach without needing a physical storefront.

Support for tech startups can create a cluster of innovation and high-paying jobs.

Strategies for Communities:
Provide training programs to help small businesses adopt digital tools and e-commerce strategies.

Develop incubators or accelerators that support tech startups and creative industries.

Partner with local schools and colleges to offer digital skills training.

Workforce Evolution and Multigenerational Dynamics

Generational shifts are reshaping the labor market and influencing economic priorities. Communities must prepare for a future workforce that values flexibility, innovation, and inclusivity.

Opportunities:
Younger workers are drawn to communities that offer a mix of professional opportunities and quality of life.

Retirees are contributing to local economies through entrepreneurship and volunteerism.

Strategies for Communities:
Offer housing and amenities that appeal to both younger workers and retirees.

Invest in education and workforce development programs that align with emerging industries.

Create programs that encourage cross-generational collaboration in businesses and civic life.

Place Branding in the Digital Age

Place branding has become more important as digital and physical worlds intersect. Communities must define and promote their unique identity to attract residents, visitors, and businesses.

Opportunities:
Authentic storytelling can set a community apart in a crowded marketplace.

Hybrid experiences, such as virtual tours paired with real-world attractions, can create broader engagement.

Strategies for Communities:
Develop branding campaigns that highlight local culture, history, and innovation.

Leverage digital platforms to showcase your community to a global audience.

Create experiences that blend digital and physical engagement, such as interactive public spaces or virtual tourism.

Technology Integration and AI-Driven Development

Advances in technology, particularly artificial intelligence, are transforming economic development strategies. Communities that embrace these tools can make smarter decisions and unlock new opportunities.

Opportunities:
AI can optimize resource allocation, forecast economic trends, and analyze community needs.

Digital tools can improve engagement, transparency, and service delivery.

Strategies for Communities:
Partner with universities or tech companies to integrate AI into economic planning.

Use data analytics to guide zoning, infrastructure, and workforce training decisions.

Provide resources for local businesses to adopt and benefit from new technologies.

Actionable Steps for Embracing Future Trends

Leverage Strengths:
Identify what makes your community unique and align it with emerging opportunities.

Highlight strengths like affordability, lifestyle, or a skilled workforce in marketing efforts.

Invest in Skills Development:
Create training programs that prepare residents for high-demand jobs in tech, digital marketing, and entrepreneurship.

Collaborate with schools, colleges, and workforce agencies to align education with market needs.

Promote Livability:
Focus on amenities that enhance quality of life, such as parks, cultural attractions, and vibrant downtowns.

Develop housing and transportation options that support a diverse and mobile workforce.

Embrace Data and Technology:
Use digital tools to monitor trends, gather feedback, and track progress. Incorporate technology into public services, engagement, and infrastructure.

Adapt Quickly:
Be willing to experiment and pivot when needed. Pilot projects and small-scale initiatives can help test new ideas without significant risk.

Looking Ahead

The future belongs to communities that anticipate change and act decisively. By focusing on trends like remote work, digital economies, and technology integration, communities can position themselves as leaders in a rapidly evolving landscape. Success will come not from following others but from defining your unique strengths and creating opportunities that align with your values and vision.

Exercise: Adapting to Remote Work

Prompt: How is remote work impacting your community? List three ways this trend is creating opportunities or challenges.

Follow-Up: What steps could your community take to attract remote workers or adapt to a distributed economy?

Exercise: Embracing Emerging Trends

Prompt: Choose one trend discussed in this chapter (e.g., digital economies, workforce evolution). How could your community position itself to take advantage of this trend?

Follow-Up: Write a short action plan with specific steps for implementation.

Kevin S. Crowder

Chapter 13:
Conclusion:
The Future of Economic Collisions

"What energy is waiting to be unlocked in your community? What collisions are ready to spark growth?"

When Dad talked about his chemistry work, he always emphasized the beauty of discovery. Every reaction, whether successful or not, taught him something new about how the world works. He believed that the process of learning, experimenting, and adapting was just as important as the outcome. This philosophy has shaped how I approach economic development. Communities, like chemical systems, are always evolving, and the most successful ones embrace that evolution with curiosity, creativity, and courage.

The principles of collision theory provide a powerful lens for understanding economic growth. Activation energy, catalysts, alignment, and equilibrium are not just abstract concepts; they are tools communities can use to create meaningful and lasting change. These principles remind us that progress is not about forcing outcomes but creating conditions where growth can happen naturally.

The Power of Small Sparks

One of the most inspiring aspects of working with communities is seeing the ripple effects of successful collisions. A small café opens on a quiet street and becomes a gathering place, inspiring other businesses to follow. A grassroots event brings people together, sparking connections that lead to new partnerships. A leader takes a bold step, and their vision ignites a movement. These moments are the building blocks of transformation, the sparks that set off growth and opportunity chain reactions.

My Dad's favorite demonstrations, like the Banana Nail or Egg in a Bottle, always showed how small adjustments could unlock extraordinary potential. In the same way, the smallest spark in a community, be it a new partnership, a pilot project, or a shared vision, can ignite a transformation that reverberates for years.

Lessons for the Future

As communities look to the future, they will face challenges that require adaptability and innovation. The principles of collision theory offer a roadmap for navigating these challenges by focusing on energy, alignment, and balance. Here are some key lessons to carry forward:

Embrace Change: Growth and progress are not static. They require constant learning, experimenting, and adjusting. Communities that are open to change will be better equipped to handle uncertainty and seize new opportunities.

Stay True to Your Identity: Just as every chemical reaction has its unique properties, every community has its own identity. Growth that aligns with this identity is far more sustainable than growth that feels imposed.

Foster Connections: Progress happens when people, businesses, and ideas collide in meaningful ways. Building trust, creating shared goals, and fostering collaboration are essential to creating these connections.

A Call to Action

The future of economic development will be shaped by those willing to experiment, collaborate, and believe in the power of connection. The tools are already in your hands. By applying the principles of activation energy, catalysts, collisions, and equilibrium, you can design systems that empower people, strengthen communities, and drive meaningful change.

As you apply the lessons of this book to your own community, I encourage you to think boldly and act deliberately; to find the will to keep going. Identify your activation energy, find your catalysts, and create the conditions for meaningful collisions. Embrace failure as part of the process, and never stop learning and adapting. Most importantly, stay true to your community's identity and values, knowing that the best growth is the kind that lifts everyone up.

Carrying the Legacy Forward

Dad used to say that the most exciting part of any experiment was the moment of possibility when everything aligned and the reaction began. I feel that same excitement when I work with communities. Nothing is more rewarding than seeing people come together, overcoming barriers, and building something greater than the sum of its parts. It is a reminder that progress, at its heart, is about connection.

Let this be your call to action: a reminder that the smallest sparks can ignite the greatest transformations. We can create systems that empower people, strengthen communities, and shape a brighter, more connected future.

Exercise: Your Community's Future Story

Imagine your community 10 years from now. What has changed? What progress has been made?

Write a short story or bullet-point outline describing your community's journey to achieve this vision. What roles did activation energy, catalysts, and alignment play in its success?

Chapter 14: Resources

Economic development requires both vision and practical tools to turn ideas into action. As with any complex system, success lies in understanding the variables, adapting to conditions, and effectively leveraging available resources. This chapter provides a toolkit for practitioners, offering templates, frameworks, and resources that align with the principles outlined in this book.

Glossary of Key Terms

Understanding the language of the chemistry of economic development is essential for collaboration and strategic planning. Below is a glossary of terms frequently used throughout this book:

Activation Energy: The initial effort or investment needed to overcome inertia and spark momentum in a community.

Catalyst: A person, policy, or program that accelerates progress by amplifying energy and creating connections.

Equilibrium: A state of balance where growth is sustainable and aligned with a community's identity and resources.

Place Branding: Creating and promoting a community's unique identity to attract residents, businesses, and visitors.

Stakeholders: Individuals or groups with an interest or investment in a community's development, including residents, businesses, and government entities.

Economic Reaction Plan Workplan:

Step 1: Assess Assets and Barriers
What are your community's unique strengths?
What challenges or inhibitors are blocking progress?

Step 2: Define Your Vision
What does success look like in 5, 10, or 20 years?
Who are the stakeholders needed to achieve this vision?

Step 3: Identify Catalysts
What small, strategic interventions can amplify existing energy?
How can these initiatives align with your community's identity?

Step 4: Measure and Sustain
What metrics will you use to track progress?
How will you ensure long-term adaptability?

Stakeholder Alignment Framework:

Goal: Bring stakeholders together to create a shared vision.

Tool: Use this framework during workshops or meetings:
- Identify individual priorities.
- Find areas of overlap and agreement.
- Develop a unified strategy based on shared goals.
- Tools for Analysis and Engagement

Data Visualization Platforms:
Tools like Street Economics™ can provide detailed insights into demographics, foot traffic, and real estate trends. These tools make complex data accessible and actionable for practitioners and stakeholders.

Community Survey Templates:
Use surveys to gather input from residents and businesses. Examples include:
- Identifying priorities for downtown revitalization.
- Measuring satisfaction with public services.
- Gathering ideas for new initiatives.

Engagement Platforms:
Platforms like Bang the Table or CivicPlus allow communities to engage residents through virtual town halls, interactive maps, and idea boards.

Exercise: Visioning for Your Community

Use this exercise to facilitate a visioning workshop with stakeholders:

Step 1: Reflect on Your Community's Identity
What makes your community unique?
What are its defining characteristics, both historical and current?

Step 2: Imagine the Future
Where do you see your community in 10 years?
What does success look like?

Step 3: Identify Key Actions
What specific steps will help achieve this vision?
Who needs to be involved, and what resources are required?

Your Practitioner's Toolkit

Economic development is as much about creativity and connection as it is about data and strategy. By using these resources, tools, and frameworks, practitioners can turn vision into action and create lasting impact in their communities.

The tools provided in this chapter are just the beginning. As you continue your work, remember that the principles of collision theory: activation energy, catalysts, alignment, and equilibrium, are always at your disposal to guide and inspire. Together, they provide a framework for growth, resilience, and transformation.

About My Dad

Gene A. Crowder, PhD

Gene A. Crowder was born Oct. 25, 1936, in Wichita Falls, Texas to Raymond and Jewel Crowder. He graduated from Blanchard (Okla.) High School and received his bachelor's degree from Central State University. He received his master's degree from the University of Florida and his Ph.D. from Oklahoma State. In 1964, he moved to Canyon Texas, where he met and married Marita Barnes, the love of his life. He was the head of the chemistry departments at West Texas State University and Louisiana Tech University, and he also served as an adjunct professor of chemistry at the University of Texas at Arlington, until 2004. He was the beloved father to Kevin and Cathryn, grandfather to Hayden and Zach, and father-in-law to Lina and T.W.

You can read more of his stories in Confessions of a Physical Chemist which is available on Amazon in eBook, paperback and hard cover.

About The Author

Kevin S. Crowder, EDP

Kevin S. Crowder is the founder of BusinessFlare® and co-founder of Street Economics™. He received the IEDC Certified Economic Developer designation in 2009 and the IEDC Certified Entrepreneurship Development Professional designation in 2021. Mr. Crowder has 30 years' experience planning and implementing economic development, including 17 years as the Director of Economic Development and Government Affairs for the City of Miami Beach and the Miami Beach Redevelopment Agency working out of the City Manager's office. Kevin is a veteran of the U.S. Army, where he served in intelligence.

One of his career highlights is his time working for the City of Miami Beach and the Miami Beach Redevelopment Agency as the Director of Economic Development and Government Affairs, leading the City's economic development program and multi-jurisdictional lobbying efforts during the Cinderella years of South Beach revitalization. He began his economic development career in 1994 with the South Beach Business Improvement Districts and the South Beach Marketing Council.

Since leaving the City of Miami Beach and establishing the BusinessFlare® brand in January 2013, Mr. Crowder has used the BusinessFlare® approach to help more than 60 communities improve their economic condition ranging in size from 1,500 to over 600,000, and last year he performed economic and fiscal analysis on projects representing more than $5 billion in private sector investment. He has further co-founded Street Economics™, an interactive economic platform for municipalities that provides actionable insights on the implementation of economic development.

He is the President of the BusinessFlare® Academy, a 501c3 not-for-profit dedicated to economic development education for local elected officials, and the co-founder of Goodnight's Red River Spice Company, a venture that celebrates American culture through food and flavor with a focus on healthy lifestyles. He has is currently integrating artificial intelligence into both his economic development and healthy lifestyle ventures.

He has authored books that include Governing for Economic Development, Gut Sandwich, Texas and Latin Comfort Food Recipes Cookbook, the Goodnight's Red River Kids Cookbook, and he published Confessions of a Physical Chemist, his father's autobiography.

Kevin S. Crowder

www.ingramcontent.com/pod-product-compliance
Lightning Source LLC
Chambersburg PA
CBHW071413220526
45469CB00004B/1279